GW01236841

Tiger Woods
Golf Great & Multi-Major Champion

by Grace Hansen

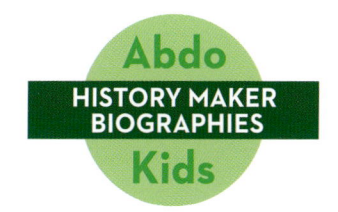

Abdo
HISTORY MAKER BIOGRAPHIES
Kids

abdobooks.com

Published by Abdo Kids, a division of ABDO, P.O. Box 398166, Minneapolis, Minnesota 55439.
Copyright © 2020 by Abdo Consulting Group, Inc. International copyrights reserved in all countries.
No part of this book may be reproduced in any form without written permission from the publisher.
Abdo Kids Jumbo™ is a trademark and logo of Abdo Kids.

Printed in the United States of America, North Mankato, Minnesota.
102019
012020

THIS BOOK CONTAINS RECYCLED MATERIALS

Photo Credits: Alamy, AP Images, Getty Images, iStock, Shutterstock, ©Shutterstock PREMIER p.13,15,17,21

Production Contributors: Teddy Borth, Jennie Forsberg, Grace Hansen
Design Contributors: Dorothy Toth, Pakou Moua

Library of Congress Control Number: 2019941235
Publisher's Cataloging-in-Publication Data

Names: Hansen, Grace, author.
Title: Tiger Woods / by Grace Hansen
Other title: Golf great & multi-major champion
Description: Minneapolis, Minnesota : Abdo Kids, 2020 | Series: History maker biographies | Includes online resources and index.
Identifiers: ISBN 9781532189043 (lib. bdg.) | ISBN 9781532189531 (ebook) | ISBN 9781098200510 (Read-to-Me ebook)
Subjects: LCSH: Woods, Tiger (Eldrick Woods)--Juvenile literature. | African American golfers--Biography--Juvenile literature. | Golfers--United States--Biography--Juvenile literature. | PGA--Juvenile literature. | Professional athletes--Biography--Juvenile literature. | Golf--United States--Juvenile literature.
Classification: DDC 796.3523 [B]--dc23

Table of Contents

Early Years 4

Going Pro 10

Making History 14

Timeline 22

Glossary 23

Index 24

Abdo Kids Code 24

Early Years

Eldrick Tont Woods was born on December 30, 1975, in Cypress, California. His father, Earl, called him Tiger from the time he was born.

5

Tiger watched Earl play golf as a toddler. One day, Earl put a golf club in his son's hands. Young Tiger swung the club and hit the ball. His dad was amazed!

7

Tiger took his first golf lesson at age 4. He kept working hard. At 16, he was invited to his first **PGA** Tour event. Tiger **birdied** his first hole!

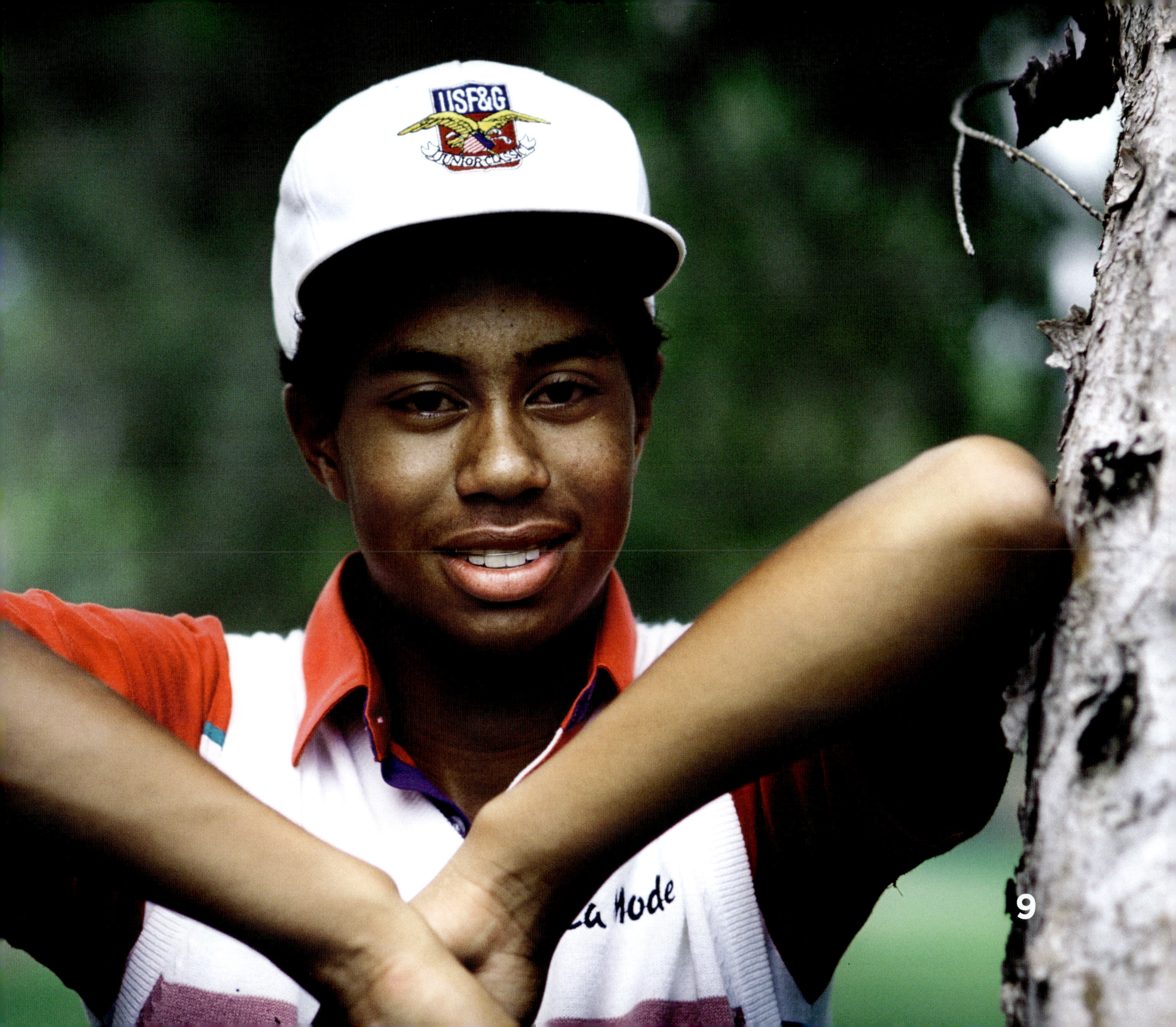
USF&G

Going Pro

By the next year, Tiger had offers from many colleges. He decided to go to Stanford University in Palo Alto, California. But after just two years there, he chose to go **pro**.

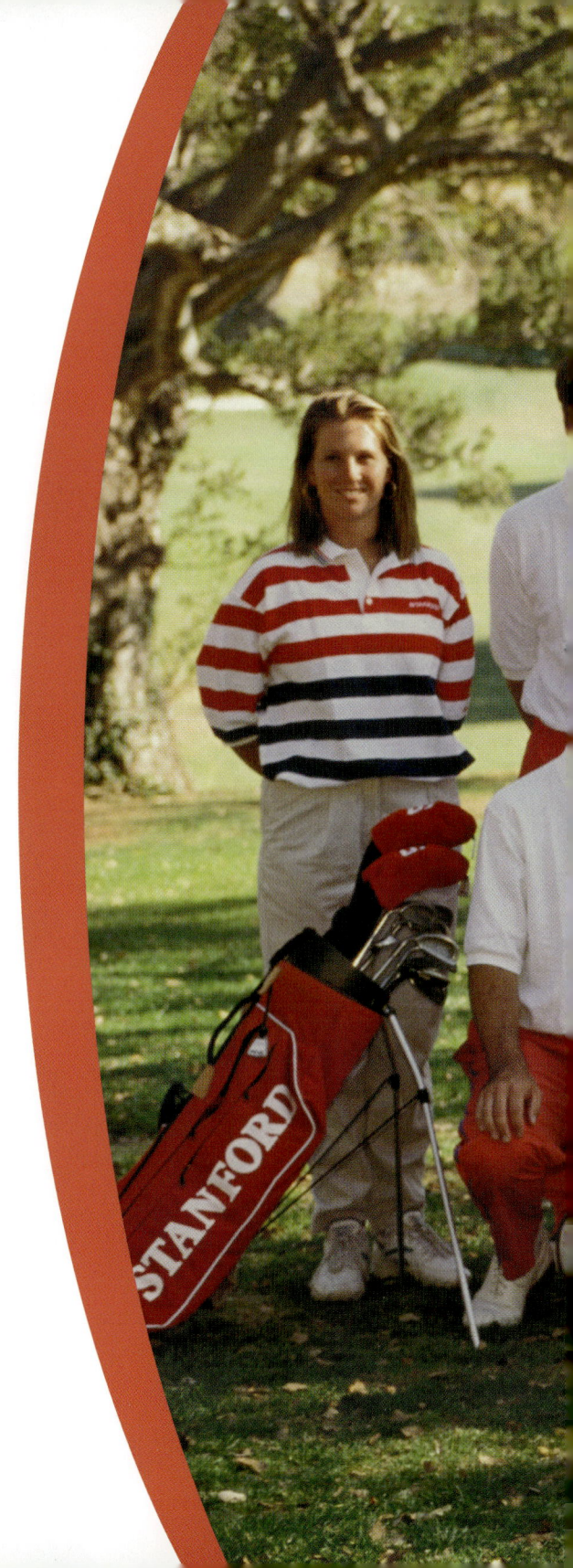

11

Before his first pro event, Tiger signed deals with Nike and Titleist. In that tournament, he made a hole in one!

13

Making History

In 1997, Tiger won the Masters Tournament at Augusta National Golf Club. He was the youngest player to do so. He was also the first black player to win the tournament.

15

In 2000, Tiger won the US Open, British Open, and **PGA** Championship. The first major in 2001 was the Masters, which Tiger won. He held the title for all four majors at one time. People called this the "Tiger Slam."

17

In 2008, Tiger began suffering from bad knee pains. Even with the pain, he won the US Open. He needed surgery to repair the damage. In 2015, he'd also need back surgery.

19

The years of pain and surgeries wore on Tiger. People didn't know if he'd ever be the same. But in 2019, Tiger won his fifth Masters Tournament. He proved that hard work can make anything possible.

21

Timeline

1975 — **December 30** Eldrick Tont Woods is born. His father nicknames him Tiger.

1996 — Tiger drops out of Stanford University to become a professional golf player.

1997 — Tiger becomes the youngest Masters winner in history and the first of African or Asian **heritage**.

2000 — Tiger wins the US Open, the **PGA** Championship, and The British Open.

2001 — Tiger wins the Masters to complete a career Grand Slam.

2007 — Tiger welcomes his first child with his wife, daughter Sam. Their son Charlie is born two years later.

2017 — In April, Tiger has his fourth back surgery. In December, he begins competing again.

2019 — Tiger wins his fifth green jacket at the Masters and his 15th major title after going 11 years without one.

Glossary

birdie – in golf, to score one stroke under par. Par is the number of strokes a golfer should need on a hole.

deal – an agreement to do business. In sports, it is often an agreement between a professional player and a brand for the player to wear, use, or represent it.

heritage – ethnic background.

PGA – an acronym for Professional Golfers' Association.

pro – short for professional.

Index

Augusta National Golf Club 14

birth 4

British Open 16

California 4, 10

education 10

family 4, 6

Georgia 14

health 18, 20

Masters 14, 16, 20

Nike 12

PGA 8, 12, 14, 16, 18

PGA Championship 16

Tiger Slam 16

Titleist 12

US Open 16, 18

Woods, Earl 4, 6

Visit **abdokids.com** to access crafts, games, videos, and more!

Use Abdo Kids code **HTK9043** or scan this QR code!